THIS IS *Lake Macquarie*

THIS IS *Lake* Macquarie

PHOTOGRAPHY BY LEO MEIER

LANSDOWNE

Published by Lansdowne Publishing Pty Ltd
Level 5, 70 George Street, Sydney NSW 2000, Australia

Published with the cooperation of the Lake Macquarie City Council

First published by Lansdowne Publishing Pty Ltd 1994

National Library of Australia Cataloguing-in-Publication Data

Meier, Leo, 1951   .
This is Lake Macquarie.

ISBN 1 86302 382 8

1. Lake Macquarie (N.S.W.) — Pictorial works. I. Title.

994.42

The photographer wishes to express his sincere thanks to Steve and Ron White
for their enthusiastic support and generous hospitality during the production of this book.

COVER:
Lake Macquarie viewed from Munibung Hill, with Eleebana Head in the background.

ENDPAPERS
A boat at anchor near Cane Point, with Belmont Bay across the water.

HALF TITLE
Morning in Cockle Bay, seen from Marmong Point at the northern end of Lake Macquarie.

TITLE SPREAD
Fishing at Lake Head.

CONTENTS SPREAD
Tranquil Cockle Bay in the early morning.

CONTENTS

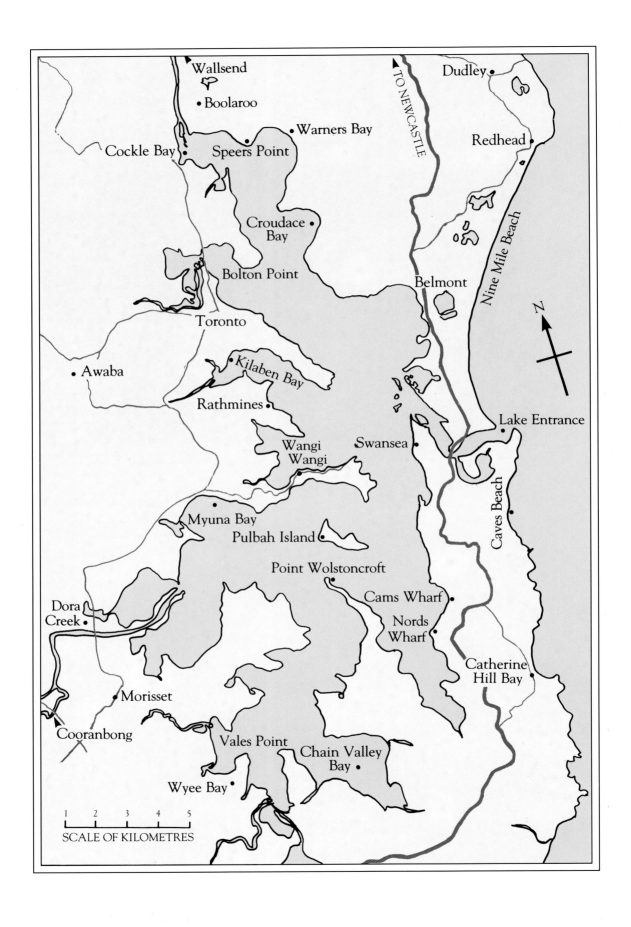

FOREWORD

The City of Lake Macquarie is centred on Australia's largest coastal lake, flanked by mountains and the Pacific Ocean.

This is a city with a unique environmental setting and an economic potential which makes it one of the most desirable areas in Australia. It has taken control of its own destiny to provide its residents with a fine future and a quality lifestyle.

Over the last twenty years, the population of Lake Macquarie has grown dramatically. This growth has enhanced the life of the community, as services, recreational amenities and excellent educational facilities have all been provided. Positive community spirit is a part of everyday living , and makes Lake Macquarie a great place to bring up children.

The protection of the native flora and fauna co-exist in harmony with the standard of living that is offered in this area. Conserving the character of the lake, preserving the natural environment, planting, improving and restoring green areas are principles that are supported by the decision makers of the City, so that the need for balance between environmental concerns and development is considered and met.

The present business structure ranges from small business to national manufacturers, providing employment opportunities for professional people, tradespersons, the semi-skilled and the unskilled. Plans for the future growth of the City encourage low-impact, high-technology industries which will provide more employment in the area and stimulate investment, to build on the quality of life already enjoyed.

The unspoiled, uncrowded conditions which provide a paradise for boating, fishing, swimming, surfing, sailing, bush walking, golfing and many other recreations and sports also promote a wide range of cultural activites. Art galleries, libraries and restaurants help give the residents of Lake Macquarie a feeling of contentment, and a unique way of life.

Lake Macquarie — the quality lifestyle.

ABOVE:
The Lake Macquarie City Council building at Boolaroo.

ON THE LAKE

Those who live by Lake Macquarie, whether they have been born and bred in this lovely region, or tempted there by the lakeside lifestyle, know that they enjoy a unique part of Australia's eastern coast; but to the traveller Lake Macquarie is always a wonderful surprise. Only a small part of it is visible from National Route 1 that bypasses the eastern shore 100 km north of Sydney, darts across the bridge at the lake Entrance at Swansea and continues on past the stunning beaches south of Newcastle. For those who stop and take a closer look, the lake has many secrets and pleasures in store.

This is one of the greatest saltwater lakes in the country: 120 square kilometres of water fed also by freshwater streams, of which Cockle and Dora Creeks in the west are the largest; 174 km of scalloped shoreline including pretty lakeside townships, lovely wooded peninsulas and secluded bays often visited only by boat.

On these habitually calm, safe waters every kind of aquatic activity is practised, from Swansea, home of the commercial fishing fleet, to the lake's sailing centre at Belmont, to the tiniest boatshed on the far shore, built to house a kids' sailing dinghy. Thousands of craft are seen on these waters. Sail-boarding, fishing, water skiing, rowing, canoeing, parasailing are popular sports, and swimmers can plunge into the lake or use the three Olympic-size pools in the region.

Created by nature, the lake has its own ecology where water fowl of many kinds thrive, and the distinctive trees and plants of the region make the lake shores beautiful in any season.

ABOVE:
Kids have their own fun while the waterskiing championships are on at Whiteheads Lagoon,
Myuna Bay.

OPPOSITE:
The tourist or day tripper can explore Lake Macquarie in a beautiful old vessel like the Wangi Queen
Showboat, which waits here at Marmong Point Marina at the northern end of the lake.

PREVIOUS PAGES:
The peaceful wooded shoreline of Moon Island Nature Reserve near the lake entrance.

ABOVE:
A yacht pushes through the Lake Macquarie Entrance, headed away from turbulent seawaters into the shelter of the second largest saltwater lake in Australia.

LEFT:
The sails of windsurfers brighten the lake as they skim around the bays. This rider is seen off Casuarina Point Reserve on the Morissett Peninsula.

OPPOSITE TOP:
In the Swansea Channel of Lake Macquarie deep-sea fishing boats and other craft head for home after a fishing expedition.

OPPOSITE BOTTOM:
This view of busy Belmont Marina and Lake Macquarie Yacht Club emphasises the importance of boating, the most popular pastime on the lake.

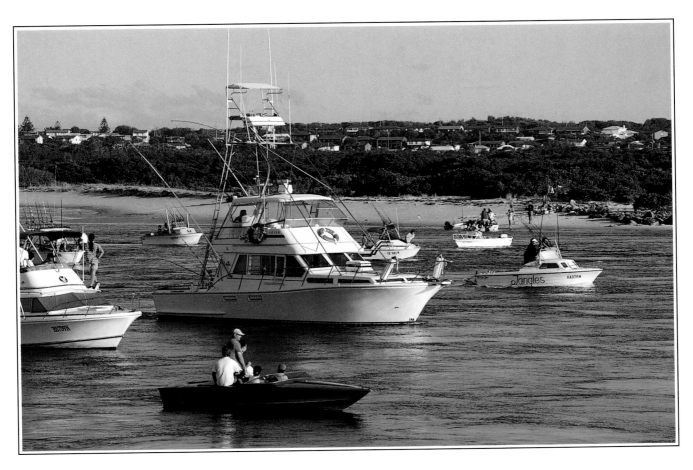

ABOVE:
A waterskier competes in the Tournament at
Myuna Bay state recreation area.

LEFT:
A high flyer takes off at Warners Bay.

ABOVE:
The lake provides a safe playground for all kinds of water sports. Here a competitor executes a spectacular jump in a New South Wales Zone 2 Open Waterskiing Tournament.

ABOVE:
Lake Macquarie is home to a wonderful variety of water birds. Here the theme is swans: wild black swans cruise together in Swan Bay at Swansea.

ABOVE:
In the late afternoon boaties enjoy some quiet fishing off Point Wolstoncroft Peninsula.

ABOVE:
Fishing can be enjoyed almost any time anywhere on this tranquil lake.

The beautiful shoreline and quiet waters of the lake make it a perfect environment for relaxing and having fun.

OPPOSITE TOP:
Business as usual on the lake as professional fishermen haul in nets near Galgabba Point on Swansea Flat. Matthew Zikman (centre) watches his son handle a fish, while Ian Fitzpatrick to his right and Greg Zikman (far right) attend to the net.

OPPOSITE BOTTOM:
Fine crabs displayed at Mannering Park Fishing Co-op, Wyee Bay.

ABOVE:
*Where bush reaches down to the lake, the shoreline provides a peaceful zone for people to enjoy,
and a habitat for wildlife.*

OPPOSITE TOP:
A pelican greets the sunrise near Wangi Wangi Park.

OPPOSITE BOTTOM:
This beautiful denizen of the lake is a white egret, on a fishing expedition in Swan Bay.

PREVIOUS PAGES:
Sunset over Lake Macquarie promises a beautiful day on the morrow.

AT THE BEACH

The City of Lake Macquarie is indeed blessed. Whilst there is no doubt that the Lake forms the heart of the region, there is another dimension of nature to enjoy. To the east of the Lake is the Pacific Ocean. The City of Lake Macquarie boasts a glorious stretch of coastline, giving the residents of Lake Macquarie the choice of a number of superb beaches.

The coastline of this region is a line of beautiful beaches, often punctuated by jagged headlands. There are smaller, intimate beaches like Dudley beach, the imposing cliffs of Redhead, the mystery of the caves at Caves beach and the open, inviting stretch of Nine Mile beach, an unbroken line of coast stretching from the entrance channel northward to Redhead.

As most of the beaches are away from the population centres, they have each retained a natural freshness not often found and as such are enjoyed all year round by the inhabitants of the City of Lake Macquarie. These beaches have everything a beach lover could ask for — crystal blue water, waves for those with energy and sun for those interested in the more gentle pursuits. Whether your wish is to ride the surf on a surf or body board, to swim in the invigorating water or simply relish the opportunity to soak up the sun away from the stress of the working week, the coastal beaches of the City of Lake Macquarie are there to be enjoyed.

Looking north across the entrance to Lake Macquarie
towards Swansea Heads.

OPPOSITE:
Looking northward from the cliffs above Caves Beach.

PREVIOUS PAGES:
Middle Camp Beach at Catherine Hill Bay, the southernmost coastal beach in the area
cared for by the City of Lake Macquarie.

ABOVE:

Popular for surfing and bathing, beautiful Caves Beach is also known for the dramatic rock formations that gave it its name.

ABOVE:
The cliffs at Redhead, as the sun rises and the moon sets.

ABOVE:
The excitement of a good wave.

OPPOSITE:
Little Redhead Point, above the magnificent surf beach of Redhead.

ABOVE:
Sand dunes behind Nine Mile Beach near Belmont, where sandmining takes place.

ABOVE:
Looking south, Redhead Beach seems
endless.

LEFT:
On the beach path at Dudley.

OPPOSITE TOP:
Sand and rolling surf on Dudley Beach, the
northernmost beach within the City of
Lake Macquarie area.

OPPOSITE BOTTOM:
Family fun on the golden sands of
Redhead Beach.

AT THE BEACH

33

Looking south from Little Redhead Point to Dudley Beach.

ABOVE:
Redhead Point cliffs tower over the coastal rocks.

IN THE MOUNTAINS

They rise majestically to the west of the Lake — the Watagan Mountains. An area of approximately 780 square kilometres, these ranges are not really mountains but a series of gently sloping ranges more like hills.

The highest point in the ranges, Mount Heaton, is contrasted with the depths of the valleys where the atmosphere is moist enough to give life to lush rainforest. Palms and ferns compete for space, looking for light, sharing their environment with tumbling waterfalls and the mosses which grow sprawling on the creek banks.

The mountains are also home to many species of birds and other wildlife, sharing this area with the many bushwalkers and campers attracted to this natural environment. There is a well-established network of trails for the nature-lover to enjoy, branching off the main roads into the lush rainforest. Although the walks are not too strenuous, for the more sedate way to enjoy nature there is always one of the many picnic spots to choose to share the environment with family and friends. Whichever way one chooses, the mountains provide a wonderful contrast to the water aspect of nature in the City of Lake Macquarie.

ABOVE & PREVIOUS PAGES:
In the State Forest near Gap Creek in the Watagan Mountains.

OPPOSITE:
The Gap Creek Falls in the state forest of the Watagan Mountains.

ABOVE:
Slender trees and lush undergrowth in the Heaton
State Forest, Sugarloaf Range.

LEFT:
This forest dweller lives in safety near the Boarding
House Dam in the Watagans.

ABOVE:
An inviting waterside walk in the Watagan State Forest.

ABOVE:
Water flows down a wooded hillside not far from the Boarding House Dam picnic area in the Watagan Mountains.

OPPOSITE:
Deep in the bush, this beautiful gum, which predates white settlement, sheds its deep red bark in gigantic ribbons.

ABOVE:
A buttress of exposed rock that forms part of the Gap Creek Falls.

ABOVE:
A picnic amongst majestic trees at Boarding House Dam in the Watagans.

OPPOSITE:
A farm nestled in the foothills of the Watagan Mountains, in Wallis Creek Valley.

ABOVE:
Children on the rural side of Lake Macquarie enjoy outdoor sports. This keen group represents the Mount Hutton Pony Club on instruction day.

ABOVE:
Golfers in the region take pleasure in the beautiful Sugar Valley golf course near West Wallsend. Mount Sugarloaf can be seen in the background.

ABOVE:

West Wallsend, a town in the foothills of the Sugarloaf Mountains, boasts a handsome public house, the Museum Hotel.

ABOVE:

The Baptist Church in Wallace Street, West Wallsend, typical of the region's early architecture.

LAKESIDE LIVING

T hose who live on the shores of Lake Macquarie are fortunate: if work demands, they can commute to nearby Newcastle or Sydney in the south, and come home each evening to relaxed living by the lake. The City of Macquarie itself is a centre for diverse industrial and commercial businesses that provide local employment beyond the long-established regional enterprises of agriculture, fishing and mining. No modern advance is lacking in this area which seems to have it all — friendly, small-town communities, city-style shopping malls, old public houses alongside up-to-date restaurants, architectural showhomes around the lake contrasting with the comfortable established houses, each with its own jetty at the bottom of the garden and a dinghy to take the family fishing.

This is a attractive environment that offers instant access to scores of leisure activities. Everyone is catered for, from the child who just likes to mess about in boats, to the retired couple who have a daily routine that may include a stroll by the lake, a trip to one of the islands in their runabout, and later a quiet drink at the local in the evenings, or dinner with friends. For the nature lover, the birds and wild creatures that share the lake with the other inhabitants have an endless fascination. In this beautiful place, there is always time to just be still and appreciate the every-changing scenery of the lake.

This is a region with its own character and pace of life, where visitors, new residents, new enterprises can take their place and share in the special experiences that only the City of Lake Macquarie provides.

ABOVE:
Houses spill down to the calm waters of Swan Bay on Marks Point.

PREVIOUS PAGES:
A view of houses nestled on the edge of Eraring Bay, taken from Fishing Point
on Lake Macquarie.

ABOVE:
The morning sun spreads over Wangi Wangi Bay, where the pleasure boats wait for their owners to take to the water.

ABOVE:
The festival to celebrate Australia Day at Lake Macquarie is held at Speers Point Park, where celebrated Australian entertainers and local cultural groups entertain the crowds.

LEFT:
An Aboriginal dancer from the Narara Dancers performs 'Altjaringa', a dreamtime corroboree, on stage at the Australia Day celebrations in Speers Point Park. Over two thousand people of Aboriginal descent are part of the population of the City of Lake Macquarie.

RIGHT:
Australia Day by the lake is one of family enjoyment and great entertainment.

BELOW:
Fireworks over the lake bring Australia Day to a close.

ABOVE:
One way of enjoying summer at Lake Macquarie: a girls' hurdle race during school athletics at Speers Point.

ABOVE:
These children prefer less strenuous fun at the Speers Point Swimming Centre.

ABOVE:

There is always the chance to admire other people's sporting efforts, as this crowd is doing at the Lake Macquarie Game Fishing Club.

ABOVE:
Easier still, for a taste of extra fresh fish you need only visit the Mannering Park Fish Co-op at Wyee Bay.

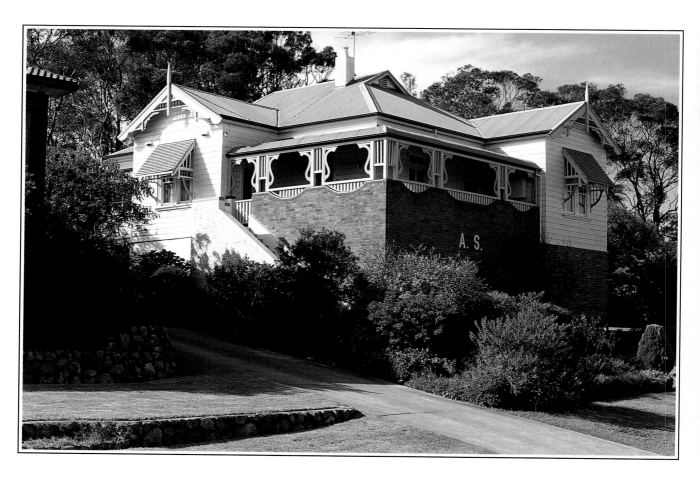

ABOVE:
Attractive architecture of the past goes well in the lakeside setting. This historic house is at No 101 Railway Street, Teralba.

ABOVE:
A touch of tradition in the lakeside town of Toronto — the historic Toronto Hotel.

ABOVE:
*For newcomers eager to adopt the Lake Macquarie lifestyle, new housing developments
are being created in the region. This one is at Caves Beach, where Spoon Rocks can be seen
in the background.*

PREVIOUS PAGES:
The site of a new development: Pinny Beach, near Cams Wharf.

ABOVE:
*Houses around Lake Macquarie are ideally adapted to the lakeside: here elevation,
the natural environment of trees, and an uninterrupted view of the lake enhance
a relaxed lifestyle.*

OPPOSITE TOP:
*Eating out on the shores of the lake induces that lazy, contented feeling ...
Here the restaurant is Ripples on the Lake, at Toronto.*

OPPOSITE BOTTOM:
*Urban buildings can be created to suit the Macquarie lifestyle. This is the distinctive
exterior of the big modern shopping complex at Charlestown.*

ABOVE:
The sun sets on another glorious day at Lake Macquarie.